FIRE TV STICK USER GUIDE: SUPPORT MADE EASY

RONALD PETER

CONTENTS

PROLOGUE

The Amazon Fire TV was released in April 2014. The Fire TV Stick was released in November 2014. Sling TV, which is going to be a necessity for cordcutters, was announced on January 4, 2015. Technology changes FAST nowadays.

To stay up to date on changes to the Fire TV Stick and learn news, tips and tricks, please sign up for updates! It's easiest to keep you informed by sending a quick email!

To sign up for updates please visit
http://www.toppingspublishing.com/firetvstick/

WHY DOES THIS BOOK EXIST?

When you open the Fire TV Stick box, there's not a lot there. The stick, a power cable, a remote, and an HDMI adapter. Amazon made this thing as simple as humanly possible - all you have to do is hook it up to your TV, right?

Everything's really simple... until it's not, and then it becomes ridiculously complicated. What if plugging it in doesn't work? What if the screen resolution isn't right? How do I watch sports shows? Why does my Fire TV Stick lose connection? Amazon has a 24x7 customer service line called Mayday that will connect you via video to an Amazon customer service representative - but it is only for Amazon tablets. The only way to get your questions about Fire TV Stick answered is to call Amazon support and wait four hours and hope they understand you, or email Amazon support and hope they understand you...or read this book!

This book is succinct. We're all busy people, so we cut right to the chase and don't repeat information. In your hands is a collection of all the tips and tricks scavenged from the deepest corners of the Internet, a few things I know myself, and a way to get the Fire TV Stick and Amazon Prime for free.

Interested yet? Keep reading! I hope you learn something in this book that makes it worth your purchase. If there is something you know about the Fire TV Stick that can help improve this book, please send an email.

Happy watching!

CUTTING THE CABLE TV CORD

Is leaving your cable TV provider behind the right decision for you? The answer depends on what you watch. Take a moment right now and think about the types of television you watch most on your TV. Is it sporting events? HBO shows? Food Network? Do you need to watch TV shows as soon as they are broadcast, or do you watch them on your own time, when it is convenient for you?

The average cable TV bill is increasing at a rate much higher than any salary increase you have seen in the past few years. According to the NPD group, the average cable bill in 2011 was $86. In 2015, the projected cable bill is $123 a month, and in 2020 the average cable bill will be $200 a month.

Purchasing the Amazon Fire TV Stick is a single part of a system that will let you stop paying for cable TV. Why pay $123 or more a month for television that you don't want to watch?

In the United States of America, TV signals are transmitted over the airwaves using ATSC (Advanced Television Systems Committee) standards. These signals are unencrypted digital television signals. They can be picked up with an HD antenna and connected to an ATSC tuner, which is probably built into your existing TV. Over-the-air broadcasts are not dead! You can probably pick up several over-the-air broadcast channels, such as ABC, NBC, CBS, FOX, CW, PBS, and other smaller networks like ION. You can get most local sports games that are on the large broadcast stations, local news, and some more popular shows - usually anything on a big network. Antennas are often quite affordable and the picture quality is excellent. The AmazonBasics antennas start at $20 for an antenna that can pick up broadcast towers within a 25 mile radius.

That brings us up to television in the 1970s. The big thing right now is streaming internet services, which is where products like the Amazon

Fire TV Stick come in. Amazon will contract with different media providers to have certain movies or television series available to their subscribers. Not all movies and TV shows are available on the same networks; Amazon, Netflix and Hulu are the biggest ones. Their media selection can vary; just because a movie is offered on Netflix one year doesn't mean the same movie will still be available on Netflix next year.

Dish Network recently announced a new service called Sling TV. Sling TV will be available in the first quarter of 2015, and will deliver several channels which were previously only available on a full cable subscription: ESPN, ESPN2, TNT, TBS, Food Network, HGTV, Travel Channel, Adult Swim, Cartoon Network, Disney Channel, ABC Family and CNN. This will be the first time ESPN is made available without a cable subscription. Sports fans rejoice, in 2016 we will be able to watch all the college bowl games again! Sling TV will cost $20/month and have no contracts or commitments.

If you have an account with these service providers, the Amazon Fire TV stick allows you to watch several services on one device. You might be thinking that all these subscriptions will add up. Let's do the math:
- Netflix streaming subscription, which provides TV shows, movies and original shows, such as House of Cards: $9
- Hulu plus subscription, which provides time-shifted access to ABC, Fox, NBC, the BBC and other networks: $8
- Amazon Prime subscription, which provides original programs such as Alpha House, HBO's back catalog, movies and many children's programs: $8.25
- Sling TV subscription, which doesn't exist yet but SOUNDS perfect for sports fans: $20

The total cost is only $45.25. HBO Go and Showtime don't exist yet as standalone subscriptions (they're coming in 2015). Even if you add these in, and allow discretionary funds for standalone TV or movie purchases, you are saving a substantial amount of money by going the Fire TV stick a la carte TV route.

FIRE TV STICK HARDWARE:
THE DIFFERENCES BETWEEN FIRE TV AND FIRE TV STICK

On a high level, the differences between the full Fire TV and Fire TV Stick are in the memory, remote control, power, and inputs.

Memory
The Fire TV Stick only offers 1 GB of memory, compared to 2 GB of memory in the Fire TV. The smaller amount of memory does not appear to affect video playback, but it may result in poor app performance. There is more memory on a Fire TV Stick than on a Roku or Chromecast.

Remote Control
Unfortunately, the remote control shipped with Fire TV Stick does not support voice search. At this time, the virtual keyboard for Fire TV Stick is alphabetical, not QWERTY, so it can take longer than usual to enter in the names of shows you want to watch. Voice search is faster and less frustrating than keyboard entry. Voice search can work immediately without any voice training, but will also learn and adjust to your voice to improve accuracy in future searches.

To get these exciting features working on Fire TV Stick, you need to purchase the "Voice remote for Amazon Fire TV and Fire TV Stick" or download the "Amazon Fire TV Remote app" for your Android or iOS device.

If you use the app, the app must first be paired with your Fire TV Stick before it will work. First, the Android or iOS device running the TV remote app must be connected to the same wireless network as the Fire TV Stick. Your phone won't be able to control anything if it can't talk to the Fire TV Stick. Launch the app, and select your Fire TV Stick to pair with. Your TV will display a code to be entered on the TV remote app. After you enter in the code, the app will be paired with your Fire TV Stick, and your device should be able to control your Fire TV Stick both as a normal remote and with voice functionality.

With a voice enabled remote, hold down the voice button to trigger voice search. You can say the movie, TV show, actor, genre, or director you are searching for. Release the voice button to trigger the search.

If you are uncomfortable with the idea of Amazon saving recordings of your voice, you can delete your voice recordings under "Manage My Device" on the Amazon web site. Deleting these recordings will make voice search less accurate for you.

Power
The Fire TV stick is powered by a micro USB cable that ends in a USB interface. In the box, there is a USB to wall socket adapter. You may be tempted to power the Fire TV Stick directly off an extra USB port on your television for simplicity or for a cleaner appearance.

There are two reasons not to do to this. First, you will be nagged constantly by your Fire TV Stick that you should plug it in directly to a wall power supply. Second, every time you turn off the TV, the Fire TV Stick is going to turn off. This means if you make a purchase at work and try to send it to your Fire TV Stick, the Fire TV Stick won't be on to receive the media file. It's more convenient in the long run to plug the Fire TV Stick into the wall.

Inputs
The Fire TV Stick has exactly 0 USB inputs while the Fire TV has a single USB input. This means if you have any peripherals, such as an external keyboard or controller, they must be Bluetooth compatible in order for the Fire TV Stick to detect them. A USB keyboard will not work with the Fire TV Stick.

Processors
The processor of the Fire TV Stick is dual core, while the processor of the Fire TV is quad core. In practice, this means a few extra

milliseconds of waiting when you are going through some menus or opening some apps, but the difference in processors is not noticable when video is playing back.

Audio
The Fire TV Stick supports Dolby Digital Plus.

THE NECESSITY OF AMAZON PRIME

To get the most out of Amazon Fire TV Stick, you definitely need to have an Amazon Prime account. Amazon Prime gives you benefits in the digital world and in the physical world.

In the digital world, you participate in Amazon Instant Video - movies or TV shows that are marked as free for Prime members can be streamed to your Fire TV Stick, iPad, Android device, iPhone, or computer web browser. If you watch a show and pause it, you can pick it up at the same place on a different device.

Second, you get access to Amazon Prime music. Amazon Prime music is a new offering that is similar to Instant Video, but for music. You get access to popular playlists and songs that can be shared across your devices, including your phone, tablets, and desktop computer.

Third, you get access to Prime Photos. Prime photos gives you an unlimited amount of storage space in Amazon Cloud drive for photos, which can display on your Amazon Fire TV stick or be shared with friends and family.

Fourth, you can borrow one book from the Kindle Owners' Lending Library each month, for free. Borrowed books do not have a due date.

There are two major benefits of Amazon Prime in the physical world as well.

The primary benefit is free two-day shipping, which was the original draw for Amazon Prime and may be the feature you are most familiar with. The secondary benefit is enormous and little known - membership sharing.

Membership Sharing

As long as you have a full Amazon Prime subscription (not Amazon Student), you can share your SHIPPING benefits with four family members. The family members do not need to have the same physical address. No other Amazon Prime benefits are shared, only 2 day shipping is sharable.

GETTING THE AMAZON FIRE TV STICK AND AMAZON PRIME FOR FREE

The easiest way to get the Amazon Fire TV Stick and Amazon Prime for free is to apply for Amazon credit cards. These offers are frequently changing; the offers discussed here are available on Amazon.com in January 2015. These credit cards are all no annual fee cards.

There are currently four credit card offers available on Amazon.com that reward you with gift certificates. If you are hesitant about carrying around too many credit cards, don't worry - we're ONLY applying for this credit card to get the Amazon.com gift certificate.

We'll discuss the four offers in order of easiest to get the gift certificate/lowest reward to hardest to get the gift certificate/highest reward. For the Discover and Citibank cards, it is worthwhile to call the credit card company to confirm your new credit card falls under the promotion you want; it is possible to get a card that does not get the promotional gift certificate. Call to confirm and be safe!

Amazon.com Rewards Visa
This card is currently offered by Chase Bank (the bank isn't always the same) and applies an instant $30 Amazon gift certificate when you are approved. Getting this gift certificate as easy as filling in the application, assuming you meet the credit score requirements. When the physical card comes in the mail, call to activate the card, then call to cancel the card immediately afterwards. When the agent asks you why you are cancelling, say "I just applied for the card to get the gift certificate." It's as simple as that.

Amazon.com Store Card
This card is currently offered by Synchrony Bank and applies an instant $40 Amazon gift certificate when you are approved. Cancelling this card

is extremely easy - the system is completely automated! You never need to talk to a person to cancel this card.

Discover it® chrome

This card is offered by Discover. After you make ONE purchase, Discover will send a $100 Amazon gift certificate by email. As soon as you get the card, make a single purchase with it. The purchase can even be an Amazon.com gift certificate to yourself for one dollar. Do not carry this card around with you - never use the card again. Put it away in a safe place. The documentation on the web site says that the gift card may take six to eight weeks to arrive, but in my experience it arrives in about four weeks. Once you get the gift certificate in the mail, apply the gift certificate to your Amazon.com account and call to cancel the card.

Citi ThankYou® Preferred Card

This card is offered by Citibank. If you make $1,000 in purchases within 3 months of getting the card, Citibank will send a $150 Amazon gift certificate by email. This gift card takes about eight weeks to arrive; follow the same principles listed above under the Discover Card.

Amex EveryDay Credit Card

This promotion is not listed on Amazon.Com. The card is offered by American Express. If you make $1,000 in purchases within 3 months of getting the card, American Express will send a promotional code for 1 free year of Amazon Prime to your email address.

EXCITED YET?

If the tips on getting Amazon gift cards for **FREE** helped you out, please leave a review of this book on Amazon!

https://www.amazon.com/review/create-review?ie=UTF8&asin=B00SGHKGSU&channel=detail-glance&nodeID=133140011&ref_=cm_cr_dp_wrt_btm&store=digital-text

SETTING UP THE FIRE TV STICK

Connect the Fire TV Stick to one of the HDMI ports on your TV. Switch the TV input to the same HDMI source the Fire TV Stick is connect to. Plug the Fire TV Stick into a wall socket, not a USB port on your TV. After you connect the Fire TV Stick to a power source, you should see a "Fire TV" splash screen. If you do not see the correct splash screen at this point, check to make sure the Fire TV Stick is receiving power.

If the Fire TV Stick is powered up, check the connections on the HDMI port to the Fire TV Stick AND the TV. HDMI is a digital signal, so it is either or not working. If the device is powered correctly, a common problem that is easily fixed is an incomplete HDMI connection.

If it is difficult to your Fire TV Stick to your TV, there is an HDMI extender included in the package. The extender plugs into your TV HDMI port, and the HDMI cable plugs into the extender and the Fire TV Stick. The HDMI extender is theoretically supposed to improve your wireless network connection. If the problem is not the length of the cable but the orientation of the cable, you can purchase a HDMI right angle adapter. When you plug the right angle adapter into a HDMI port, it will move the available HDMI port ninety degrees, which may be more accessible for the Fire TV Stick.

Insert 2 AAA batteries (included) and press the play button. You should see a change on the TV screen. If nothing happens on the TV, press the Home button for a few seconds, then press the play button.

Your Fire TV Stick will begin to scan for a local wireless network. A wireless network connection is essential for the Fire TV Stick to function. Select your network from the list of available networks, and enter your network password if applicable. If your Fire TV Stick cannot connect to your network, try both the 2.4 GHz or 5.0 GHz frequency of your router.

When the Fire TV Stick makes a network connection, you will be asked to create a new Amazon account if you do not have one already. If you purchased the Fire TV Stick from Amazon, and you are the user, your account information will be prepopulated. Make sure you change the account information if the Fire TV Stick was purchased under one user's account, but will be used under a different user's account.

Finally a short video from Amazon will play, explaining how the remote works, how streaming works, and a few choices for mobile apps.

The Fire TV Stick does not require a "Smart TV" to work; it only needs a free HDMI port to connect. It is not tied down to one TV. You should be able to set it up on one TV, watch some shows, then move it to a different TV and continue watching. It is limited by the network connection, so the places you want to use it in your home should have both a TV with a free HDMI port and a strong wireless signal.

At this time, it will be difficult to use the Fire TV Stick in a hotel room on the road. Most modern hotels have TVs with free HDMI ports; the issue is wireless connectivity. In almost every hotel the way you connect your computer to the Internet is by accessing a special web page to confirm you are a hotel customer, logging in, and having your computer authorized to connect to the hotel's wireless network. Currently there is no way for the Fire TV Stick to confirm this authorization.

Different Country, U.S. Based Amazon Prime Account
Fire TV Stick will technically work in the United Kingdom and Germany, but your purchased and rented U.S. videos will no longer be accessible. To do this, you have to switch the address for your Amazon account to the UK or Germany, deregister your Fire TV Stick, and reregister your Fire TV Stick. You're not going to be accessing all your U.S. Amazon content in Germany - it's more like having a Fire TV Stick FROM Germany. Some games and apps may not work at all - your mileage may vary.

Searching

Searching will sort through a large database of terms. You can search by genre or actor, Amazon content, apps, and titles within apps. For example, you can search for the Netflix app. You can also search for "Transformers", which might be specific in your mind, but ambiguous to Amazon. Searching for "Transformers" may bring up movies you can buy and download from Amazon, temporarily free movies for Amazon Prime members, or apps which have Transformers content in them.

Replacing the Remote Battery

To some, this seems silly, but a large number of users have problems replacing the battery on the remote.

There is a rectangle on the back of the remote, in the middle. Next to the rectangle, there is an edge where the battery cover meets the remote. Put your thumb on the rectangle, press down gently, and push the rectangle away from the edge.

Universal Remotes

You may have a lot of electronics connected to your TV, and want to use your preexisting universal remote to control your Fire TV Stick. Beware - infrared remote controls will not work with the Fire TV Stick.
If your universal remote is Bluetooth capable, you can use it for your Fire TV Stick. Logitech's Harmony Hub creates a Bluetooth connection for Harmony Home products, so if you happen to have this remote already, you are in luck. The Harmony Hub and Harmony Home products are confirmed working with both Fire TV and Fire TV Stick: http://support.myharmony.com/en/harmony-experience-with-amazon-fire-tv

Parental Controls

There are two types of parental controls offered for Amazon Fire TV and Amazon Fire TV Stick. Only one works with Fire TV Stick!

PIN-based Parental Controls

The parental controls on a Fire TV Stick are PIN-based. There is one PIN for the entire device. There are a few different settings you can configure to make them require a PIN to continue. You can require a PIN for all purchases, only require a PIN for Instant Video, or block broad categories of content. Examples of these content categories are apps, games, music, and photos.

Let's give a real world example: You want to allow a child to play Minecraft, but be able to do nothing else on the Fire TV Stick. The way you would do this is to install ONLY the Minecraft app and lock everything except for apps. This way, a child will only be able to use Minecraft and will be prompted for a password to access any other function on the Fire TV Stick.

Configure your PIN settings through Settings -> Parental Controls.

Using a PIN-based system is easy, but it offers less flexibility than per user restrictions. Let's say one of your kids wants to buy an app or watch a movie right now and you're busy. All it takes is one time of you shouting out "Here's the PIN!" and now your children can do whatever they want to do on the device...unless you go back and change the PIN, then the whole cycle starts again, now you've forgotten your PIN...This system is definitely better than nothing, as long as you are aware that FreeTime does not work with the Fire TV Stick.

Amazon FreeTime
FreeTime is a service provided by Amazon that gives a parent or caregiver extremely detailed control over the Fire TV experience for 1 to 4 children. It offers a well-curated walled garden for children that can be filled with kid-safe media and has an easy to navigate menu.

A profile is set up for each child. In the profile, you can set time limits on the amount of Fire TV a profile can watch videos or use apps each day. You can also set a bedtime; after bedtime, the profile will not be able to use media on the Fire TV anymore. You can customize which movies, TV shows, and apps appear on each profile.

FreeTime gives the Fire TV user the ability to highly customize a children's experience, at the cost of becoming a systems administrator for the household.

Amazon offers a paid upgrade to FreeTime called FreeTime Unlimited. FreeTime Unlimited is a prepacked set of movies, TV shows, books and apps that have been preapproved by Amazon as being child safe. FreeTime Unlimited lets you have most of the benefits of FreeTime, without paying the penalty of picking and choosing each thing your child is allowed to do.

FreeTime is only available for Amazon Fire TV; it is not available for Fire TV Stick.

Removing Recently Watched Items

The main menu of Fire TV Stick shows the most recently used apps, games, movies, or TV shows watched. This is great if you want a shortcut to a game you play all the time, or if you want to resume watching a movie that you paused, but it's not so great if you don't want your children or your spouse to know you were watching something. If you want to remove an item, from the home screen, select Recent and move to the item you want to delete. Select "Remove from Recent".

Deleting the ASAP cache

Advance Streaming and Prediction (ASAP) is not mentioned prominently in the Fire TV Stick documentation. ASAP is Amazon's recommendation engine. It runs in Amazon's cloud, processes its catalog of content, applies what it thinks it knows about you, and will predict which TV shows or movies you are most likely to watch. Fire TV Stick then predownloads the media onto the Fire TV Stick. Once the media is on the Fire TV Stick, it can be watched instantly, without waiting for a download to start from Amazon's servers.

If you are security and privacy sensitive, unfortunately, there is no way to disable the ASAP feature.

The ASAP cache is stored on the 8 GB of local space on Fire TV Stick. If you need to clear this cache to free up space for new games or apps, go to Settings -> Applications -> Amazon Video -> Clear Cache. In this menu, you can also clear the cache for any apps.

WAYS TO WATCH ON
AMAZON FIRE TV STICK

This section will list a series of ways to watch TV and movies or subscribe to different channels.

In general, you will need a subscription to access the content from streaming services through Fire TV Stick. For example, you must have an existing Netflix subscription (or create a new one) to use the Netflix app.

You do not **need** to have an Amazon Prime subscription (but it's nice!) If you have purchased items through Amazon Instant Video, and viewed them on a different device, you will still be able to stream that content over your Fire TV Stick without having an Amazon Prime subscription. Movies purchased digitally from the Amazon store will show up in your library automatically for streaming. The primary advantage of having Amazon Prime is that it makes the experience more user-friendly and integrated. Amazon designed the Fire TV Stick system assuming that the user would have Amazon Prime, so everything works more smoothly with Prime.

HBO GO is available for Fire TV, but not yet available for Fire TV Stick. HBO GO should be available in Spring 2015 for Fire TV Stick, right around the time that HBO's standalone subscription is available. The standalone subscription will give access to HBO television shows directly through HBO. Currently, you need to subscribe to HBO through a cable provider to use HBO GO; when the standalone subscription arrives, you will be able to pay only for HBO channels directly to HBO, not for a full cable package.

The most difficult shows for cordcutters to watch have always been live sporting events. Until Sling TV goes live, the only way to watch ESPN on Fire TV STick is if you have an existing cable subscription. The following providers offer access to ESPN via the WatchESPN app:

- AT&T U-verse
- Bright House Networks
- Charter
- Comcast XFINITY
- Cox
- DISH
- Google Fiber
- Midcontinent Communications
- Optimum
- Time Warner Cable
- Verizon FiOS TV

WatchESPN offers access to some MLB games. MLB offers its own app called MLB.TV, which offers subscription access to all MLB games, with restrictions. Oddly enough, the restrictions are for teams local to your zip code! For example, if you live in Los Angeles, you can watch live games for all OTHER teams except the Dodgers and Angels. In-market games are available 90 minutes after the actual baseball game is completed.

Be aware of the limitations of each streaming content app!

Sling TV
The CEO of Sling TV, Roger Lynch, revealed some additional information on the service on January 15, 2015.

Sling TV pricing is month-to-month and does not require a contract to use. The cost of Sling TV is $20/month. The subscription will give you live access to ESPN, ESPN2, CNN, TBS, TNT, HGTV, Food Network, Cartoon Network, Adult Swim, Travel Channel, ABC Family, Maker, and the Disney Channel.

There are two $5 add-ons.

The first $5 add-on is called "News and Info Extra". This package contains HLN, DIY, Bloomberg, and the Cooking Channel.

The second $5 add-on is called "Kids Extra". This package contains Boomerang, Baby TV, Duck TV, Disney Junior, and Disney XD.

A "Sports Extra" package is in the works, but details (such as which channels will be included) have not been finalized. Sling TV will definitely give access to WatchESPN functionality.

Local content (which can be accessed over the air with an antenna) is not currently part of Sling TV. According to Lynch, "one of our core tenets is not forcing subscribers to pay for channels that are already getting for free."

If you want to use Sling TV on devices besides Fire TV Stick, you can install Sling TV, but only one device at a time can be actively streaming Sling TV.

If bandwidth or hitting your data cap is a concern, you will be able to limit the bandwidth available for Sling TV to stream data.

You can sign up for an early invitation for Sling TV at Sling.com.

I WANT TO WATCH MY OWN
MOVIE COLLECTION ON TV

Perhaps you already have an extensive movie collection you have converted to digital, and you just want to watch your own videos and movies that are stored on a computer connected to your network.

The Fire TV Stick is powerful enough to play 1080p high quality movies without lag over the wireless connection. The issue is connecting the Fire TV Stick to your media files.

There are two common solutions to this problem: Plex and Kodi. Plex is simpler to set up in the beginning, but is more difficult to maintain in the long run. XBMC is the reverse; it is more difficult to set up in the beginning, but once everything is set up and working, it is very easy to watch your shows or movies.

Plex

Plex needs two parts to work: an official Plex app, and a server the Plex app connects with to deliver media to the Fire TV Stick. A desktop or laptop computer can work as the server, but it must on at the same time your Fire TV Stick is using Plex to look for the movie. The hardware requirements for Plex are higher than if you select the Kodi solution.

One additional expense to consider is multitasking on the Plex server computer. If you do not have a computer dedicated to your home theater, the performance of the Plex server may be inhibited by the constant transcoding of videos - this will make the computer slower if someone is using it to perform other operations.

Kodi

Kodi plays media by connecting to network shares. It does not require any additional software running on a computer to play movies, but it does require some computer sharing a folder of movies over the

25

network. You can play files directly from any local or network connection - it is possible to load movie files directly onto the Fire TV Stick.

The most difficult part about using Kodi is getting it onto the Fire TV Stick. The process of loading Android apps onto the Fire TV Stick is called SIDELOADING. It may feel intimidating, but you can complete the process of sideloading Kodi in about 10 minutes.

SIDELOADING

There are four steps in sideloading an app such as Kodi to the Fire TV Stick. This process requires using a computer connected to the same network as the Fire TV Stick. The steps are: enable Android Debug Bridge (ADB), get the IP address of the Fire TV Stick, install ADB for Windows, and finally installing the desired app.

To enable ADB debugging, Settings -> System -> Developer Options -> Enable ADB Debugging.

To get the IP address of the Fire TV Stick, Settings -> System -> About -> Network. Write down the IP address.

On your Windows computer, install ADB for Windows.

Finally, download the app you wish to install (it should end with the suffix APK). In a command prompt window, type in

adb connect IPADDRESS
adb install C:\filepath\filename.apk

The app will be accessible from the home menu under Settings -> Applications.

Common apps to sideload are web browsers and game emulators.

PHOTOS

If you have Amazon Prime, a new benefit is Prime Photos. Prime Photos offers unlimited photo storage in your Amazon Cloud drive for your photos. When you use the Amazon Photos app for iPhone or the Amazon Cloud Drive Photos app for Android to sync the photos taken on your phone or tablet with your Amazon Cloud drive, your personal photos will be available anywhere you can access Amazon Cloud, such as your Fire TV Stick.

You can see stored images in your Cloud Drive on your Fire TV Stick, or take photos with your phone and have them displayed on your TV almost instantly.

Fire TV Stick has the option of showing a screensaver. The screensaver can show photos from your Amazon Cloud Drive account or photos from Amazon.

While the default screensaver functions without any problems, there were issues with the mosaic screensaver at launch, and it is not clear if these issues have been resolved or not. The default screensaver on the Fire TV Stick shows a slideshow of images, one image after another. The mosaic screensaver shows a series of images combined into a grid format. When the mosaic screensaver is selected, images from Amazon are not cached. Each time the screensaver shows a new image, the image is downloaded from the Amazon Cloud to your Fire TV Stick. This results in abnormally high data use over your Internet connection. Stay away from the mosaic screensaver until this issue has been confirmed to be fixed.

MUSIC

There are two categories of music that are playable through your Fire TV Stick - songs from your music library, and songs from Amazon Prime.

The Amazon Music Libary is populated in different ways. You can think of it like a digital cloud storage locker that you upload your songs to. Once the songs are in your Music Library, they can be listened to on whatever device (phone, tablet, computer) that can run the Amazon Music app.

In 2013 Amazon announced AutoRip. AutoRip simultaneously added an MP3 copy of each song on a CD to your Music Library whenever you bought a CD. Even better, Amazon went back in time, looked at your music purchase history since 1998, and added MP3 copies of each of THOSE songs to your Music Library. You may have not known Amazon Music Library existed before this moment, but your Music Library has always been there in the cloud, waiting for you to listen to it.

To summarize, your Music Library is a combination of songs you actively decide to put in the Music Library, and songs that are passively added by Amazon when you purchase a CD.

The other category of music on a Fire TV Stick is Amazon Prime Music. To use this feature, you must be an Amazon Prime member. There is not currently a way to add Prime Music songs or playlists to your Music Library on a Fire TV Stick; you must add Prime Music through a desktop computer or a phone/tablet.

To add Prime Music songs or playlists, go to www.amazon.com/primemusic on a supported device. After you add Prime music to your library, it will be playable on your Fire TV Stick.

From the Home Screen, select Music. Everything in your Music Library will be displayed, from songs you put there yourself to Prime music added from your computer or phone.

Don't forget about voice search - if you have a voice remote, or downloaded the app to your phone, you can search your music by saying the name of the artist, album title, playlist name, or song.

You can shuffle songs within an individual playlist or songs within an album, but you cannot shuffle all your Prime Music at once. You are only authorized to listen to Prime Music on one device at a time, so if you are using your Amazon Fire TV Stick you cannot simultaneously listen on your phone.

For some songs, lyrics will be available and displayed on the TV while the music is playing. Songs that have lyrics available are labelled "Lyrics" next to the song title. Lyrics are timed to the song playback and displayed line by line. Lyrics may be available for songs that have been added to your Music Library through the digital music store or songs that have been uploaded by you to your Music Library and automatically matched by Amazon to a song in the digital music store catalog.

GAMING ON THE
AMAZON FIRE TV STICK

The Fire TV Stick is not intended to compete with full game consoles. Instead, gaming is an additional feature for a device that is primarily intended to stream media. Not all games will be playable on the Fire TV Stick; simple mobile games work best, and game performance is noticeably slower than on the Fire TV. Mobile Android games and some party games work well in the living room location of the Fire TV Stick.

Controllers

Any Bluetooth controller should be compatible with the Amazon Fire TV stick. Wired controllers will not work (remember, there is no USB port) and wireless 2.4 GHz controllers will not work.

The Nyko Playpad Pro for Amazon Fire TV is a compatible controller for $20.

The OUYA Wireless Controller is available at $35. OUYA is a separate gaming console, but the controller is Bluetooth based and will pair with the Fire TV stick as "OUYA Game Controller".

The Playstation Dualshock 4 controller is Bluetooth compatible and will work with Amazon Fire TV stick out of the box. The Playstation home button is already configured to go to the Fire TV Stick home screen.

If you have any Bluetooth controller at home already, attempt to pair it with the Fire TV stick before purchasing any new solution. The official game controller is the most expensive option at $40.

All Bluetooth controllers follow a similar syncing process to the Fire TV Stick.

Select "Settings" from the home menu and go to the "Controllers" section on the right. Select "Controllers", then "Bluetooth Game Controllers".

On the next screen, select "Add Bluetooth Controllers".

This makes the Fire TV Stick begin searching for nearby Bluetooth devices to pair with. On your Bluetooth controller, hold down the pairing button until the Fire TV Stick synchronizes with the controller.

The controller may be identified as a generic "Gamepad" initially, but as information is exchanged between the controller and the Fire TV Stick, a more accurate name will be displayed on the Fire TV Stick.

After your controller is paired, confirm all the buttons are working correctly.

GameCircle

Amazon's GameCircle provides leaderboards for game scores and is a way for players to measure their game performance against people all over the world. It has all modern features of social gaming, with the ability to have named friends, and can also syncronize game saves, achievements, and leaderboard information across different devices.

INSTALLING AND CONFIGURING APPS

App Installation

By default, only Amazon apps are installed on Fire TV Stick. Any other app, such as Netflix or Hulu, must be downloaded to your Amazon account.

If you find browsing the Fire TV Stick App Store on a TV frustrating, there is another method for getting apps onto your Fire TV Stick. Browse the Amazon Appstore with your desktop computer. When you buy an app, you can select the delivery location to your Fire TV Stick. After you purchase the app on your desktop, the app installation will be pushed out.

Play Media From Your Phone or Computer on the TV

It's easy to take photos and record video from your phone or tablet now, but we still like VIEWING the media we create on a large screen television. The problem is that it is cumbersome to move the picture or video from your phone to something that can display it on the TV. With the assistance of local media sharing apps, Fire TV Stick can bridge the gap between your phone and TV. This process can also show pictures or videos stored on your computer on your television.

Allcast is a solution that will display photos, videos, and music on your Android device through a Fire TV Stick onto your TV. Allcast comes in two parts - an app for your Android device downloadable through Google Play, and a companion receiver app for the Fire TV Stick. When both applications are installed, Allcast on your portable Android device will automatically start the receiver app on the Fire TV Stick when you are ready to start streaming media.

Plex does a lot more than Allcast, but requires a separate computer that is on and connected to your network. The installation process is similar to Allcast - you install an app on Fire TV Stick, and an app on your phone/tablet, but a third piece of Plex server software is part of the installation package.

Mirroring for Android

If your phone or tablet is Miracast compatible, you can mirror its screen on the Fire TV Stick. The simplest integration is between devices in Amazon's ecosystem such as the Fire TV tablet or Fire phone. To enable screen mirroring, on your Fire TV Stick, go to Settings -> Display & Sounds, then select "Enable Wireless Mirroring".

Next, from your phone or tablet, go to "Display", then "Display Mirroring"/"Share Your Screen via Miracast". Your Fire TV Stick will show up as an option. Once you select to mirror your screen to the Fire TV Stick, it may take 20 seconds for your phone or tablet data to show up on your TV.

Mirroring for iOS (via AirPlay)

The AirPlay system from Apple is intended to stream content from an iPhone, iPad, or Mac desktop onto your TV through Apple TV. This functionality can be replicated on a Fire TV Stick through third party applications.

AirPlay emulation works best with pictures or audio. Streaming videos via emulated AirPlay on a Fire TV Stick is going to be slow, lag, and have buffering issues. Video playback may also be limited by your local network capacity. AirPlay can work directly from some iOS apps but not apps will be compatible.

There are several apps that will simulate AirPlay; the most popular one is AirPlay/DLNA Receiver (PRO).

Third-Party App Installation

Apps for Fire TV Stick in the Amazon app store are only a fraction of the software that is available. Since Fire TV Stick is Android based, almost any Android app that can be used with a remote control should be compatible. The term used for putting an app onto your Fire TV Stick that is not from the Amazon app store is SIDELOADING.

Some sources of third-party apps can be dangerous, so you have to use your own judgement when determining if a third-party app is safe for you to download or not. The most common vector for infecting iPhones and iPads is when they are jailbroken, and apps containing bad stuff are downloaded from a third-party app lister of ill repute.

Sideloaded apps will not show up on the Fire TV Stick home screen. The third-party apps are visible under Settings -> Applications.

TROUBLESHOOTING

There are two common troubleshooting techniques with the Amazon Fire TV Stick: reboot, and check the network connection.

The simplest way to reboot the Fire TV Stick is to unplug the power cord from the stick, wait three seconds, then plug the power cord back in. Rebooting should always be the first troubleshooting step for a Fire TV Stick problem.

If rebooting doesn't solve the problem, there is a long list of problems that all have to do with network connectivity. Just like your computer, phone, or tablet, the Fire TV Stick needs to be able to connect to the Internet in order to function properly.

The HDMI extender included with the Fire TV stick allows the Fire TV Stick to be moved farther away from any electronics which may interfere with the wireless signal from your router to the Fire TV Stick. Try using the HDMI extender and a long HDMI cable instead of plugging the Fire TV Stick directly into the television.

Purchased and downloaded content is tied to a specific Amazon account. If a movie was downloaded under one account, and the Fire TV stick is currently registered to a different user, the Fire TV Stick will not decode and play the movie. To change the registered user of the Fire TV Stick, go to the Home screen, select Settings, and then select My Account. Select the current account and Deregister it. Register the original account to enable playback of the downloaded movies.

For remote problems, reboot the Fire TV Stick first, then check the batteries on the remote.

Wireless Connectivity Troubleshooting Steps
Make sure the power source for the Fire TV Stick is coming from a wall socket, not a USB port on the television or some other USB port. The

Fire TV Stick can use more power than amount provided over a USB port.

Move your router closer to the Fire TV Stick.

Unplug your router and your modem. Wait 60 seconds. Plug in your modem, and wait another 60 seconds. Plug in your router, and wait another 60 seconds. Reboot your Fire TV Stick.

If your router broadcasts on both the 2.4 GHz and 5.0 GHz frequencies, switch to the one that is not in use.

Check the wireless network password on the Fire TV Stick.

Video Playback Issues
Clearing application data may resolve some video playback issues such as "Error 13".

From the Home screen, select Settings -> Applications -> Manage All Installed Applications. Select the application you want to clear the data for. Select "Force Stop", then "Clear Data". When prompted to Delete App Data, select Clear Data again.

Once the application data is cleared, reboot the Fire TV Stick. You may need to enter account login information again to play the video.

EPILOGUE

If this book was helpful to you, please leave a review of this book on Amazon! Every review helps!

https://www.amazon.com/review/create-review?ie=UTF8&asin=B00SGHKGSU&channel=detail-glance&nodeID=133140011&ref_=cm_cr_dp_wrt_btm&store=digital-text

One last time - for the latest news on Fire TV Stick please sign up for updates! It's easiest to keep you informed via email!

To sign up for updates please visit
http://www.toppingspublishing.com/firetvstick/

OTHER BOOKS BY RONALD PETER

TV Without Cable: Guide to Free Internet TV and Over-the-Air Free TV

Tired of Comcast, Dish, or DirectTV?
We're on hold with them for hours, and if we're lucky enough to get a representative who speaks English, they schedule an appointment two weeks in the future. Why does paying for cable services cost over $100/month?

Wondering What the Best Setup Is For Home?
Every day new services or devices are announced, each one promising to make our lives better and simpler. They all sound the same - do you want to have a detailed comparison and recommended setups for your living room TV?

In this book, we'll talk about ways you can watch the shows you want to watch, whenever you want to watch them. Movies, television, and sports!

Buy TV Without Cable: Guide to Free Internet TV and Over-the-Air Free TV on Amazon.com; http://www.amazon.com/gp/product/B00STRA2SG

www.ingramcontent.com/pod-product-compliance
Lightning Source LLC
Chambersburg PA
CBHW060934050326
40689CB00013B/3083